~A BINGO BOOK~

Psychology Bingo Book

COMPLETE BINGO GAME IN A BOOK

Written By Rebecca Stark
Educational Books 'n' Bingo

ISBN 978-087386-449-7

Educational Books 'n' Bingo

Printed in the U.S.A.

PSYCHOLOGY BINGO DIRECTIONS

INCLUDED:

List of Terms

Templates for Additional Terms and Clues

2 Clues per Term

30 Unique Bingo Cards

Markers

1. **Either cut apart the book or make copies of ALL the sheets. You might want to make an extra copy of the clue sheets to use for introduction and review. Keep the sheets in an envelope for easy reuse.**

2. Cut apart the call cards with terms and clues.

3. Pass out one bingo card per student. There are enough for a class of 30.

4. Pass out markers. You may cut apart the markers included in this book or use any other small items of your choice.

5. Decide whether or not you will require the entire card to be filled. Requiring the entire card to be filled provides a better review. However, if you have a short time to fill, you may prefer to have them do the just the border or some other format. Tell the class before you begin what is required.

6. There are 50 terms. Read the list before you begin. If there are any terms that have not been covered in class, you may want to read to the students the term and clues before you begin.

7. There is a blank space in the middle of each card. You can instruct the students to use it as a free space or you can write in answers to cover terms not included. Of course, in this case you would create your own clues. (Templates provided.)

8. Shuffle the cards and place them in a pile. Two or three clues are provided for each term. If you plan to play the game with the same group more than once, you might want to choose a different clue for each game. If not, you may choose to use more than one clue.

9. Be sure to keep the cards you have used for the present game in a separate pile. When a student calls, "Bingo," he or she will have to verify that the correct answers are on his or her card AND that the markers were placed in response to the proper questions. Pull out the cards that are on the student's card keeping them in the order they were used in the game. Read each clue as it was given and ask the student to identify the correct answer from his or her card.

10. If the student has the correct answers on the card AND has shown that they were marked in response to the *correct questions,* then that student is the winner and the game is over. If the student does not have the correct answers on the card OR he or she marked the answers in response to *the wrong questions,* then the game continues until there is a proper winner.

11. If you want to play again, reshuffle the cards and begin again.

Have fun!

TERMS

AGGRESSION

ASC (Altered States of Consciousness)

ANXIETY DISORDERS

ASSIMILATION

BEHAVIOR

CATHARSIS

CHUNKING

CLASSICAL CONDITIONING

COGNITIVE

CONFORMITY

DEFENSE MECHANISMS

DELUSIONS

DSM

EMPATHY

FEAR

SIGMUND FREUD

FRUSTRATION

FUNCTIONAL FIXEDNESS (Fixity)

GESTALT PRINCIPLES

HIERARCHY OF NEEDS

HYPOCHONDRIA

ILLUSIONS

INTELLIGENCE

INTERNALIZATION

CARL JUNG

LEARNING

MEMORY

MOOD DISORDERS

MULTIPLE INTELLIGENCES

NARCISSISTIC PERSONALITY DISORDER

NERVOUS SYSTEM

NEURON

PERSONAL SPACE

PERSONALITY

PHOBIA

PREJUDICE

PROBLEM SOLVING

PSYCHOLOGIST

PSYCHOLOGY

PSYCHOTHERAPY

PSYCHOTIC DISORDERS

REASONING

REINFORCEMENT

SCHIZOPHRENIA

SELF-ACTUALIZATION

SLEEP DISORDERS

B.F. SKINNER

SOCIOPATH

TRIAL & ERROR

TRANSFERENCE

Additional Terms

Choose as many additional topics as you would like and write them in the squares. Repeat each as desired.
Cut out the squares and randomly distribute them to the class.
Instruct the students to place their square on the center space of their card.

Clues for Additional Terms

Write three clues for each of your additional terms.

_____	_____
1.	1.
2.	2.
3.	3.
_____	_____
1.	1.
2.	2.
3.	3.
_____	_____
1.	1.
2.	2.
3.	3.

© **Barbara M. Peller**

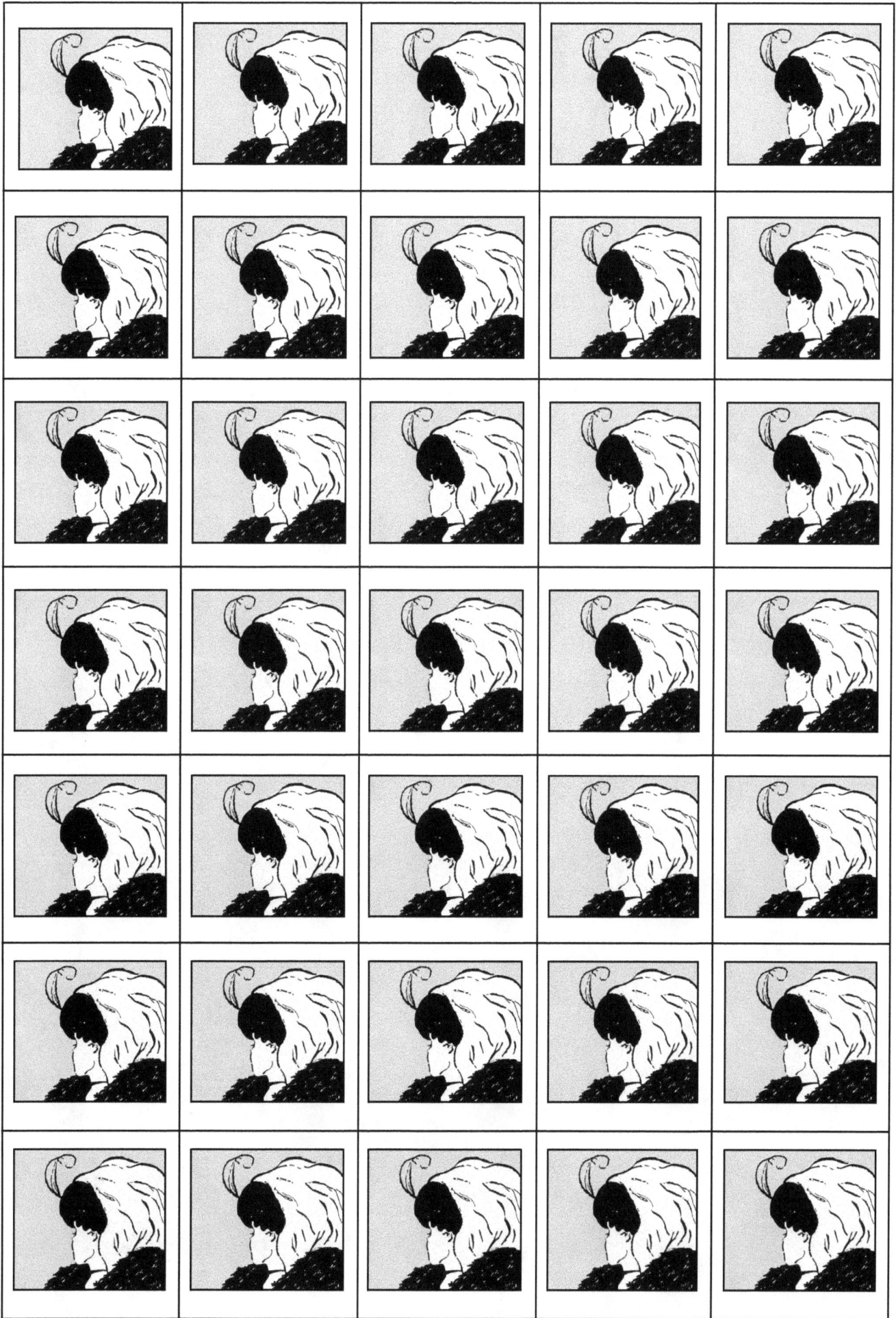

AGGRESSION
1. This type of behavior is intended to cause harm or pain.
2. This hostile behavior can be verbal, physical or mental.
3. It does not include behavior that accidentally causes harm or pain.

ASC (Altered States of Consciousness)
1. Dreaming is the most common one.
2. Nightmares, including incubus nightmares, are very disturbing ones.
3. Hypnosis is one that is induced by a person whose suggestions are readily accepted by the subject.

ANXIETY DISORDERS
1. These are characterized by a lot of worry and tension even when there is little or nothing to provoke the intense emotional response.
2. Obsessive-Compulsive Disorder is an example. It is characterized by recurrent, unwanted thoughts and/or repetitive behaviors.
3. Panic disorder is one in which sufferers experience unexpected, severe panic attacks.

ASSIMILATION
1. It is the process by which we take in new information and incorporate it into existing ways of thinking.
2. It is the opposite of accommodation, the process of changing existing ideas to adapt to new information.
3. According to Jean Piaget, this and accommodation are the 2 sides of adaptation.

BEHAVIOR
1. This refers to the actions and reactions of an organism as it adjusts to its environment.
2. Principles of learning are used to improve this.
3. Positive and negative reinforcement are some techniques used to modify this.

CATHARSIS
1. This is the process of expressing strong, but repressed emotions.
2. First used by Josef Breuer, this term comes from a Greek word meaning "to purge."
3. Breuer used this process to rid patients of their symptoms by having them recall traumatic experiences and expressing the original emotions that had been repressed & forgotten.

CHUNKING
1. This mnemonic device takes single items of information and organizes them into units.
2. This memory technique can help us remember telephone numbers.
3. Because short-term memory is limited, this technique helps us process long bits of information.

CLASSICAL CONDITIONING
1. This process elicits a behavior through a stimulus that has acquires its powerthrough its association with a biologically important stimulus.
2. A well-known example is when Pavlov got dogs to salivate in response to a bell first by ringing the bell with food present and then by ringing it alone.
3. In this type of behavior modification, the elicited behavior is the conditioned response.

COGNITIVE
1. This refers to the process of being aware, knowing, thinking, learning and evaluating.
2. This type of therapy treatment tries to change feelings and behaviors by changing the way the person *thinks about* his or her life experiences.
3. These processes include perception, language, problem solving and abstract thinking.

Psychology Bingo

CONFORMITY
1. This is the degree to which members of a group will change their behavior, views and attitudes to fit the views of the group.
2. This process influences the formation and maintenance of social norms.
3. Peer pressure often encourages this type of behavior.

DEFENSE MECHANISMS
1. These psychological strategies allow people to cope with reality and to maintain self-image.
2. An example is repression, or excluding desires and impulses from one's consciousness and trying to keep them in the subconscious.
3. An example is projection, the attributing of one's own unacceptable or unwanted thoughts or/and emotions to others.

DELUSIONS
1. These clearly false beliefs are held in spite of evidence to the contrary.
2. With grandiose ___ the individual believes that he or she has special powers, talents, or abilities or that he or she is a famous person.
3. Persecutory ___ are the most common type. The individual believes he or she is being harassed, followed, or otherwise "persecuted."

DSM
1. The full name of this text is *Diagnostic and Statistical Manual of Mental Disorders*.
2. This manual covers all mental health disorders for both children and adults. It includes diagnostic criteria as well as known causes.
3. The first edition of this guide that classifies mental disorders was published in 1952.

EMPATHY
1. This is the capacity to understand another's state of mind or emotion. Although similar to sympathy, it is not the same.
2. Someone who has the ability to "put himself in another's shoes" is said to have this.
3. It is the ability to imagine oneself in another's place and understand the other's feelings, desires, ideas, and actions.

FEAR
1. Like joy, anger, and grief, this is a primary emotion.
2. An irrational, intense, and persistent one is called a phobia.
3. Unlike anxiety, which may occur without any external threat, this is an emotional response to danger.

SIGMUND FREUD
1. Born in what is now the Czech Republic and raised in Vienna, this physician is often called the "Father of Psychoanalysis."
2. According to his views, the human personality comprises three principal systems: the id, the ego and the superego.
3. His technique of psychoanalysis involved free association and dream analysis.

FRUSTRATION
1. This emotion occurs in situations where one is blocked from reaching a personal goal.
2. The more important the goal that is blocked, the greater the ___.
3. Aggression is a possible effect of this emotion. It may be a direct attack on the obstacle or, if the obstacle can not be identified, the anger might be generalized.

FUNCTIONAL FIXEDNESS (FIXITY)
1. Karl Duncker used this term in 1945 to describe the tendency of people to regard a particular object as having one, fixed function.
2. This can hinder problem solving if a new use of a familiar object is necessary.
3. To demonstrate it, Duncker asked subjects to use a candle, a box of nails, and matches to attach the candle to the wall so that it did not drip on the table.

GESTALT PRINCIPLES OF GROUPING
1. These include similarity, proximity, continuity, and closure.
2. One of the principles, continuity, refers to the tendency to perceive things as belonging together if they form a continuous pattern.
3. One of the principles, closure, refers to the tendency to complete familiar objects that have gaps in them.

Psychology Bingo

HIERARCHY OF NEEDS
1. Abraham Maslow believed that needs at each level in a ___ must be met before the next level can be achieved.
2. Maslow said that physiological ones were the most basic in the ___.
3. According to Maslow, self-actualization was the highest level in the ___ .

© Barbara M. Peller

HYPOCHONDRIA
1. People with this disorder are convinced that even minor physical symptoms mean that they have a serious disease or illness.
2. Sufferers of this disorder do not believe doctors or medical tests that say they are in good health.
3. People with this disorder often think they have a disease after reading or hearing about it.

ILLUSIONS
1. Optical ones are the most common.
2. Unlike hallucinations, which are distortions in the absence of a stimulus, these are misinterpretations of real sensations.
3. These distort the senses in a manner usually shared by others in the same environment.

INTELLIGENCE
1. It includes such abilities as the ability to learn, to adapt to new situations, to deal with complex and abstract material, to perceive spatial relations and to be creative.
2. The Binet-Simon test measures this.
3. An individual's ___ Quotient is expressed by dividing the mental age by the chronological age and multiplying by 100.

INTERNALIZATION
1. This process involves an individual's acceptance of the norms established by people who are influential to him or her.
2. This is more likely to occur if a role model is seen as endorsing a particular set of norms.
3. The process involves learning what the norms are, understanding why they are of value, and then accepting the norm as one's own viewpoint.

CARL JUNG
1. This Swiss psychologist is known as the "Founder of Analytical Psychology."
2. He coined the term "collective unconscious."
3. He said that archetypes are innate universal psychic dispositions that enable us to act like humans.

LEARNING
1. It is a relatively permanent change in behavior or knowledge that results from experience or training.
2. A synonym is "conditioning."
3. Behavioral modification, especially through experience or conditioning, can be called this.

MEMORY
1. This is the mental capacity to encode, store and retrieve information.
2. It is usually divided into three storage systems: sensory, short-term, and long-term.
3. Amnesia is the lack of this.

MOOD DISORDERS
1. Two of the most common ones are depression and bipolar disorder.
2. Serotonin and norepinephrine, which allow brain cells to communicate with one another, are implicated in the one known as depression.
3. The one known as bipolar disorder is characterized by extreme mood swings.

MULTIPLE INTELLIGENCES
1. This educational theory was first developed by Howard Gardner.
2. Gardner's categories of this included Bodily-Kinesthetic, Interpersonal, Verbal-Linguistic, Logical-Mathematical, Naturalistic, Intrapersonal, Spatial, and Musical.
3. According to this theory there are seven different ways to demonstrate intellectual ability.

NARCISSISTIC PERSONALITY DISORDER
1. This disorder is characterized by a grandiose sense of self importance, an excessive need for admiration, and a lack of empathy.
2. People who suffer from this have an inflated sense of their own importance and think they are better than others.
3. Beneath their feelings self-importance, people with this disorder often have a fragile self-esteem.

Psychology Bingo

© Barbara M. Peller

NERVOUS SYSTEM 1. The central ___ comprises the brain and the spinal cord. 2. The peripheral ___ is divided into the somatic and the autonomic. 3. The somatic ___ is associated with voluntary control of body movements; the autonomic acts to maintain normal internal functions and is not subject to voluntary control.	**NEURON** 1. This is the basic unit of the nervous system.Its nucleus is enclosed in the soma, or cell body. 2. It is a cell specialized to receive, process, and/or transmit information to another cell. 3. The area where the axon terminal of one comes close to the dendritic zone of another is called a synapse.
PERSONAL SPACE 1. This refers to the space surrounding one's body that a person considers private. 2. The amount that is preferred varies from culture to culture and situation to situation. 3. If this is entered by another person without the individual desiring it, it makes the individual feel uncomfortable.	**PERSONALITY** 1. Psychologists describe an individual's ___ in terms of types and traits. 2. It may be broadly defined as an individual's distinctive way of thinking, feeling and behaving. 3. The MMPI (Minnesota Multiphasic ___ Inventory), the Rorschach Inkblot Test, and the Thematic Apperception Test (TAT) are frequently used to assess this.
PHOBIA 1. This common anxiety disorder is an irrational, intense, and persistent fear of a situation, activity, thing, or person. 2. An extreme or irrational fear of heights, is called acro___. 3. The fear of open spaces or of being in crowded, public areas is called agora___.	**PREJUDICE** 1. This is a learned negative attitude toward objects or people. 2. The beliefs used to that justify this learned negative attitude are in the form of stereotypes, or generalizations in which certain characteristics are assigned to all members of a group. 3. It is an irrational negative attitude towards an individual, a group, or a race.
PROBLEM SOLVING 1. This higher-level thinking begins with the discovery that a problem exists. 2. During this process the individual may suddenly realize what he or she thinks is the solution. This is sometimes called "insight" or the "aha!" experience. 3. The last stage in this is verification of the solution. If it is proved correct, the process is over.	**PSYCHOLOGIST** 1. This type of professional is a specialist in the study of the structure and function of the brain and related behaviors or mental processes. 2. A ___ can only use talk therapy as treatment; he or she cannot prescribe medication. 3. This person is trained and educated to perform psychological research, testing, and therapy.
PSYCHOLOGY 1. It is the study of the mind and mental processes, especially in relation to behavior. 2. Social ___ looks at how the actions of others influence the behavior of an individual. 3. Clinical ___ focuses on the diagnosis and treatment of disorders of the brain, emotional disturbances, and behavior problems.	**PSYCHOTHERAPY** 1. It is a way of treating mental and emotional disorders by talking about the condition and related issues with a mental-health professional. 2. Some types of this treatment focus on changing current behavior patterns. 3. Some types of this treatment focus on understanding past issues.
Psychology Bingo	© **Barbara M. Peller**

PSYCHOTIC DISORDERS 1. When symptoms are severe, people with these disorders have difficulty staying in touch with reality and often are unable to meet the ordinary demands of daily life. 2. The major symptoms of these disorders are hallucinations and delusions. 3. Schizophrenia is an example of this type of disorder.	**REASONING** 1. This is the process of thinking in which conclusions are drawn from a set of facts. 2. Deductive ___ moves from given statements which are assumed to be true, called premises, to conclusions, which must be true if the premises are true. 3. Inductive ___ makes generalizations based on some specific observations.
REINFORCEMENT 1. There are four types: positive, negative, punishment, and extinction. 2. Positive ___ , the most powerful type, adds something in order to increase a response. 3. Negative ___ takes something negative away in order to increase a response.	**SCHIZOPHRENIA** 1. This is a psychotic disorder. Symptoms include hallucinations, delusions, thought disorder, and disorders of movement. 2. It is a chronic, severe, and disabling brain disorder that affects about 1% of Americans. 3. ___ is a severe brain disorder in which people do not interpret reality in a normal manner.
SELF-ACTUALIZATION 1. In Abraham Maslow's hierarchy of needs theory, this is the final level of psychological development. 2. According to Maslow, this level is achieved when all basic and meta needs are fulfilled. 3. It may be defined as "the full realization of one's potential."	**SLEEP DISORDERS** 1. These are chronic disturbances in the amount or quality of sleep that interfere with a person's ability to function normally. 2. Insomnia is one in which the individual is unable to fall asleep or stay asleep or wakes before getting enough sleep. 3. Sleepwalking, or somnambulism, is one.
B.F. SKINNER 1. He invented the operant-conditioning chamber. 2. His most famous experiments involved a pigeon. When the pigeon made the correct response, it was rewarded with a pellet of food. 3. He called the type of learning he demonstrated with the pigeon "opererant conditioning."	**SOCIOPATH** 1. This person suffers from an antisocial personality disorder. He or she is manipulative and never recognizes the rights of others. 2. This person is a pathological liar and lacks remorse, shame or guilt. He or she exhibits other antisocial behaviors as well. 3. A ___ lacks a conscious. Although he or she can be charming, it would only be for self-gain.
EDWARD LEE THORNDIKE 1. He is known as the "Father of Educational Psychology." 2. His classic example of S-R (stimulus-response) theory was a cat learning to escape from a "puzzle box" by pressing a lever inside the box. 3. His "puzzle box" showed that animals learn by trial & error and that transfer of learning occurs because of previously encountered situations. Psychology Bingo	**TRANSFERENCE** 1. It is the redirection of feelings and desires, especially of those unconsciously retained from childhood, toward a new object 2. It is the redirection of the client's feelings toward a person in his or her past to the therapist. 3. A therapist can use this unconscious redirection of feelings to reveal unresolved conflicts with people from the client's childhood. © Barbara M. Peller

Psychology Bingo

Frustration	Aggression	Catharsis	Internalization	Mood Disorders
Chunking	ASC	B.F. Skinner	Neuron	Multiple Intelligences
Anxiety Disorders	Transference		Phobia	Defense Mechanisms
Reinforcement	Sigmund Freud	Trial & Error	Memory	Personal Space
Problem Solving	Hierarchy of Needs	Psychology	Sociopath	Self-Actualization

Psychology Bingo

Reinforcement	Anxiety Disorders	Nervous System	Schizophrenia	Intelligence
Personal Space	DSM	Assimilation	Sigmund Freud	Memory
Delusions	Hierarchy of Needs		Functional Fixedness	Trial & Error
Reasoning	Psychotic Disorders	Transference	Psychologist	Self-Actualization
Multiple Intelligences	B.F. Skinner	Psychologist	Chunking	Sociopath

Psychology Bingo: Card No. 2

© Barbara M. Peller

Psychology Bingo

Reinforcement	Trial & Error	DSM	Memory	Anxiety Disorders
Neuron	ASC	Conformity	Aggression	Carl Jung
Sigmund Freud	B.F. Skinner		Learning	Behavior
Transference	Delusions	Problem Solving	Reasoning	Nervous System
Sociopath	Chunking	Psychology	Psychologist	Intelligence

Psychology Bingo: Card No. 3

Psychology Bingo

Transference	Learning	Catharsis	Chunking	Intelligence
Narcissistic Personality Disorder	Classical Conditioning	Aggression	Schizophrenia	Anxiety Disorders
Phobia	Reasoning		Mood Disorders	Internalization
Trial & Error	Empathy	B.F. Skinner	Psychologist	Assimilation
Cognitive	Multiple Intelligences	Prejudice	Sociopath	Defense Mechanisms

Psychology Bingo: Card No. 4

Psychology Bingo

Multiple Intelligences	Mood Disorders	Sigmund Freud	Assimilation	Chunking
Narcissistic Personality Disorder	Trial & Error	Conformity	Functional Fixedness	ASC
Catharsis	Defense Mechanisms		Neuron	Hypochondria
Self-Actualization	Intelligence	Frustration	Psychologist	Fear
DSM	Psychology	Anxiety Disorders	Transference	Phobia

Psychology Bingo: Card No. 5

Psychology Bingo

Behavior	Memory	Nervous System	Intelligence	Defense Mechanisms
Learning	Sigmund Freud	Fear	Aggression	Anxiety Disorders
Schizophrenia	Cognitive		Classical Conditioning	Functional Fixedness
Psychologist	Problem Solving	Psychology	Prejudice	Catharsis
Personal Space	Assimilation	Frustration	Phobia	Empathy

Psychology Bingo: Card No. 6

Psychology Bingo

Frustration	Memory	Hypochondria	Neuron	DSM
Personal Space	Intelligence	Hierarchy of Needs	ASC	Narcissistic Personality Disorder
Nervous System	Internalization		Functional Fixedness	Classical Conditioning
Transference	Reasoning	Conformity	Reinforcement	Delusions
Psychologist	Chunking	Psychology	Prejudice	Behavior

Psychology Bingo: Card No. 7

Psychology Bingo

Phobia	Learning	Gestalt Principles	Memory	Classical Conditioning
Narcissistic Personality Disorder	Catharsis	Schizophrenia	Defense Mechanisms	Assimilation
Empathy	Psychotherapy		Intelligence	Mood Disorders
Sociopath	Transference	Reinforcement	Cognitive	Reasoning
B.F. Skinner	Psychology	Prejudice	Sigmund Freud	Personal Space

Psychology Bingo

Functional Fixedness	DSM	Hierarchy of Needs	Empathy	Chunking
Cognitive	Intelligence	Phobia	Sigmund Freud	Learning
Carl Jung	Frustration		ASC	Gestalt Principles
Fear	Self-Actualization	Problem Solving	Neuron	Hypochondria
Reasoning	Psychologist	Conformity	Reinforcement	Mood Disorders

Psychology Bingo

Reinforcement	Memory	Classical Conditioning	Schizophrenia	Empathy
Defense Mechanisms	Assimilation	Aggression	ASC	Intelligence
Psychotherapy	Learning		Internalization	Delusions
Problem Solving	Self-Actualization	Fear	Psychology	Carl Jung
Conformity	Personal Space	Nervous System	Multiple Intelligences	Phobia

Psychology Bingo

Behavior	Learning	Sigmund Freud	Fear	Personal Space
Gestalt Principles	Carl Jung	Neuron	Functional Fixedness	Aggression
Narcissistic Personality Disorder	Intelligence		Nervous System	Hierarchy of Needs
Conformity	Anxiety Disorders	Psychologist	Chunking	Reinforcement
Cognitive	Psychology	Frustration	Prejudice	DSM

Psychology Bingo: Card No. 11

© Barbara M. Peller

Psychology Bingo

DSM	Mood Disorders	Carl Jung	Memory	Functional Fixedness
Hierarchy of Needs	Personal Space	Catharsis	Prejudice	ASC
Frustration	Hypochondria		Defense Mechanisms	Schizophrenia
Psychology	Reasoning	Intelligence	Reinforcement	Narcissistic Personality Disorder
Learning	Gestalt Principles	Psychotherapy	Cognitive	Assimilation

Psychology Bingo: Card No. 12

Psychology Bingo

Fear	Mood Disorders	Behavior	Carl Jung	Defense Mechanisms
Catharsis	Gestalt Principles	Intelligence	Functional Fixedness	Delusions
Learning	DSM		Hierarchy of Needs	Hypochondria
Phobia	Psychologist	Classical Conditioning	Psychotherapy	Reinforcement
Psychology	Self-Actualization	Prejudice	Frustration	Neuron

Psychology Bingo: Card No. 13

Psychology Bingo

Chunking	Intelligence	Sigmund Freud	Functional Fixedness	Cognitive
Assimilation	Frustration	Carl Jung	ASC	Learning
Fear	Internalization		Nervous System	Conformity
Self-Actualization	Psychologist	Psychotherapy	Classical Conditioning	Behavior
Psychology	Schizophrenia	Delusions	Personal Space	Phobia

Psychology Bingo

Neuron	Functional Fixedness	Sigmund Freud	DSM	Memory
Behavior	Nervous System	Aggression	Catharsis	Cognitive
Defense Mechanisms	Frustration		Anxiety Disorders	Learning
Psychology	Carl Jung	Gestalt Principles	Psychologist	Fear
Personal Space	Reasoning	Prejudice	Empathy	Hierarchy of Needs

Psychology Bingo

Classical Conditioning	Carl Jung	Gestalt Principles	Empathy	Psychotic Disorders
Schizophrenia	Delusions	Hypochondria	Narcissistic Personality Disorder	Internalization
Fear	Mood Disorders		Defense Mechanisms	Hierarchy of Needs
Transference	Assimilation	Psychology	Personality	Reinforcement
Cognitive	Sleep Disorders	Prejudice	Reasoning	Learning

Psychology Bingo

Conformity	Personality	Illusions	Carl Jung	Chunking
Neuron	Cognitive	Psychologist	Internalization	Hypochondria
Functional Fixedness	Phobia		Sleep Disorders	Gestalt Principles
Self-Actualization	Personal Space	Reinforcement	Sigmund Freud	Delusions
Problem Solving	Fear	DSM	Learning	Mood Disorders

Psychology Bingo

Empathy	Psychotherapy	Assimilation	Fear	Schizophrenia
Learning	Conformity	Problem Solving	Defense Mechanisms	Cognitive
Functional Fixedness	Delusions		Illusions	Catharsis
Self-Actualization	Aggression	Psychologist	Reinforcement	Nervous System
Sleep Disorders	Carl Jung	Sigmund Freud	Personality	Behavior

Psychology Bingo: Card No. 18

© Barbara M. Peller

Psychology Bingo

Defense Mechanisms	Behavior	Carl Jung	Gestalt Principles	Defense Mechanisms
Neuron	Learning	Memory	DSM	Internalization
Personality	Chunking		ASC	Anxiety Disorders
Nervous System	Sleep Disorders	Problem Solving	Reasoning	Illusions
Catharsis	Psychotic Disorders	Personal Space	Phobia	Prejudice

Psychology Bingo

Psychotherapy	Personality	Memory	Carl Jung	Prejudice
Assimilation	Hierarchy of Needs	Narcissistic Personality Disorder	Problem Solving	Schizophrenia
Mood Disorders	Hypochondria		Transference	Aggression
Multiple Intelligences	B.F. Skinner	Sociopath	Reasoning	Sleep Disorders
Trial & Error	Phobia	Psychotic Disorders	Reinforcement	Illusions

Psychology Bingo

Neuron	Behavior	Narcissistic Personality Disorder	Carl Jung	Multiple Intelligences
Mood Disorders	Illusions	Classical Conditioning	Gestalt Principles	Frustration
Delusions	Personal Space		Personality	Sigmund Freud
Problem Solving	DSM	Sleep Disorders	Self-Actualization	Phobia
Transference	Psychotic Disorders	Prejudice	Conformity	Reasoning

Psychology Bingo: Card No. 21

© Barbara M. Peller

Psychology Bingo

Empathy	Nervous System	Illusions	Catharsis	Fear
Schizophrenia	Memory	Anxiety Disorders	Gestalt Principles	ASC
Assimilation	Internalization		Frustration	Hypochondria
Sleep Disorders	Self-Actualization	Reasoning	Aggression	Chunking
Psychotic Disorders	Conformity	Personality	Delusions	Narcissistic Personality Disorder

Psychology Bingo

Classical Conditioning	Personality	DSM	Catharsis	Prejudice
Behavior	Psychotherapy	Personal Space	Neuron	Aggression
Nervous System	Fear		Sociopath	Frustration
Delusions	Psychotic Disorders	Sleep Disorders	Conformity	Reasoning
Multiple Intelligences	B.F. Skinner	Phobia	Problem Solving	Illusions

Psychology Bingo

Classical Conditioning	Psychotherapy	Chunking	Personality	Gestalt Principles
Illusions	Prejudice	Narcissistic Personality Disorder	Schizophrenia	Frustration
Hypochondria	Empathy		Fear	Delusions
Multiple Intelligences	Sociopath	Sleep Disorders	Conformity	Mood Disorders
Trial & Error	Transference	Psychotic Disorders	Memory	B.F. Skinner

Psychology Bingo: Card No. 24

© Barbara M. Peller

Psychology Bingo

Transference	Narcissistic Personality Disorder	Personality	Sigmund Freud	Illusions
Aggression	Self-Actualization	Neuron	Classical Conditioning	ASC
Mood Disorders	Gestalt Principles		Sociopath	Sleep Disorders
Anxiety Disorders	Multiple Intelligences	B.F. Skinner	Psychotic Disorders	Internalization
Prejudice	Chunking	Cognitive	Assimilation	Trial & Error

Psychology Bingo

Illusions	Personality	Nervous System	Schizophrenia	Empathy
Problem Solving	Memory	Gestalt Principles	Psychotherapy	Classical Conditioning
Self-Actualization	Sociopath		Internalization	Transference
Conformity	Catharsis	Multiple Intelligences	Psychotic Disorders	Sleep Disorders
Hypochondria	Cognitive	Sigmund Freud	B.F. Skinner	Trial & Error

Psychology Bingo

Nervous System	Assimilation	Personality	Psychotherapy	Hierarchy of Needs
Multiple Intelligences	Sociopath	Neuron	Sleep Disorders	ASC
Psychology	B.F. Skinner		Psychotic Disorders	Transference
Empathy	Behavior	Narcissistic Personality Disorder	Trial & Error	Aggression
Cognitive	Internalization	Illusions	Anxiety Disorders	Hypochondria

Psychology Bingo

Defense Mechanisms	Psychotherapy	Anxiety Disorders	Personality	Classical Conditioning
Hierarchy of Needs	Illusions	Sociopath	Schizophrenia	Internalization
B.F. Skinner	Delusions		Hypochondria	Problem Solving
Reinforcement	Empathy	Personal Space	Psychotic Disorders	Sleep Disorders
Catharsis	Functional Fixedness	Cognitive	Trial & Error	Multiple Intelligences

Psychology Bingo: Card No. 28

Psychology Bingo

Illusions	Psychotherapy	Empathy	Neuron	Functional Fixedness
Self-Actualization	Problem Solving	Narcissistic Personality Disorder	Hypochondria	Anxiety Disorders
Mood Disorders	Sociopath		ASC	Personality
Hierarchy of Needs	Multiple Intelligences	Intelligence	Psychotic Disorders	Sleep Disorders
Classical Conditioning	Gestalt Principles	Trial & Error	Behavior	B.F. Skinner

Psychology Bingo: Card No. 29

Psychology Bingo

Chunking	Personality	Schizophrenia	Functional Fixedness	Sleep Disorders
Aggression	Psychotherapy	Nervous System	Internalization	ASC
Self-Actualization	Fear		Hypochondria	Narcissistic Personality Disorder
Trial & Error	Behavior	Catharsis	Psychotic Disorders	Sociopath
Multiple Intelligences	DSM	B.F. Skinner	Illusions	Anxiety Disorders

Psychology Bingo: Card No. 30

www.ingramcontent.com/pod-product-compliance
Lightning Source LLC
Chambersburg PA
CBHW050442300326
41934CB00043B/3316